THE HARVEST GYPSIES

THE
HARVEST GYPSIES

ON THE ROAD TO THE GRAPES OF WRATH

JOHN STEINBECK

INTRODUCTION BY CHARLES WOLLENBERG

HEYDAY, BERKELEY, CALIFORNIA

Originally published in conjunction with Santa Clara University as part of the California Legacy series.

Library of Congress Number: 88203891
ISBN: 978-1-890771-61-4

Photographs from the archives of the Farm Security Administration, reprinted courtesy of the Bancroft Library, University of California, Berkeley.

Cover Photo: Migrants on the road, February 1936, by Dorothea Lange
Cover Design: Ashley Ingram
Book Design: Sarah Levin
Printed in Canada by Hignell Book Printing on recycled paper (100% post consumer waste).

Published by Heyday
P.O. Box 9145, Berkeley, California 94709
(510) 549-3564
heydaybooks.com

20

INTRODUCTION

Charles Wollenberg

JOHN STEINBECK WROTE HIS MASTERPIECE, *The Grapes of Wrath*, in 1939, dedicating it to "Carol, who willed this book," and to "Tom, who lived it." "Carol" was Carol Henning Steinbeck, the author's wife; "Tom" was Tom Collins, manager of a federal migrant labor camp in the California Central Valley.

Steinbeck met Collins three years earlier, in 1936, shortly after *The San Francisco News* hired the author to write the series of articles gathered in this volume (originally published in the News, October 5-12, 1936). While accompanying Steinbeck on a tour of the "Hoovervilles" and "Little Oklahomas" of rural California, Collins provided him with much of the in-depth knowledge that makes this series compelling reading even fifty years after the fact. In the process, Tom Collins helped launch John Steinbeck on a personal and literary journey that would lead to the publication of *The Grapes of Wrath*.

Steinbeck received the *News* offer just as he was experiencing some long-delayed fame and fortune. Born in Salinas in 1902, he dreamed of becoming a writer while still at Salinas High School. He entered Stanford, but left in 1925 without a degree. In the years that followed he failed to make a living as a writer and was forced to take various short-term jobs and accept financial help from his family. By the early 1930s Steinbeck had matured into a big, rough-hewn man who masked his considerable sensitivities and insecurities behind a gruff, hard-drinking exterior.

With the publication of *Tortilla Flat* in 1935 his fortunes finally changed. In this funny, satirical novel about a group of down-and-out Mexican Americans Steinbeck turned to his roots in the Salinas Valley and Monterey. The book was immensely popular, although it was criticized by middle class Monterey burghers who objected to its off-beat depiction of their community, and, in later years, by Chicano activists who believed it played on unfavorable Latino stereotypes.

By the time *Tortilla Flat* was published, Steinbeck was at work on a far more serious book. He had met an organizer for the Communist Party's Cannery and Agricultural Workers Industrial Union, which in 1933 had launched an ambitious, though ultimately unsuccessful, attempt to organize California farm laborers. Steinbeck used the organizer's experiences as the basis for *In Dubious Battle*, a grim story of a farm workers' strike. The book was generally well-received, in spite of grower criticisms of its pro-worker perspective and radical unease at its less-than-flattering portrayal of Communist organizers. *In Dubious Battle* established John Steinbeck's reputation as a serious writer with expertise on farm labor matters.

Steinbeck had met George West, an editor for *The San Francisco News,* some years earlier at the Carmel home of the noted radical journalist, Lincoln Steffens. After *In Dubious Battle* was published, West asked the writer to do a series on the dust bowl migration then sweeping through rural California. Steinbeck eagerly accepted and in the summer of 1936 began touring the state's agricultural valleys in an old bakery truck. The federal Resettlement Administration, a New Deal agency that was beginning to establish camps for migrant workers, was looking for favorable publicity and assigned a staff member to accompany the author. It was at the agency's Weedpatch Camp at Arvin, in Kern County, that Steinbeck first encountered Tom Collins.

Collins was the model for the fictional Jim Rawley, manager of the government "Wheatpatch Camp" in *The Grapes of Wrath*. Ma Joad, matriarch of the Okie family whose experiences form the core of the novel, saw Rawley as a "little man dressedall in white . . . a man with a thin, brown, lined face and merry eyes. He was lean as a picket. His white clean clothes were frayed at the seams." Steinbeck described the real-life Collins similarly, adding that he looked "tired beyond sleepiness, the kind of tired that won't let you sleep even if you have time and a bed." Collins had previously been a teacher in Guam, the director of a school for delinquent boys, and a social worker for the Federal Transient Service, which dispensed emergency relief in the early Depression years. He joined the Resettlement Administration in 1935, managing the agency's first migrant camp at Marysville. When Steinbeck met him, he was in the process of establishing the Resettlement Administration's second facility at Arvin. JacksonBenson, Steinbeck's major biographer, called Collins "an idealist, a utopian reformer, a romantic, yet also a good administrator."

Steinbeck stayed at Weedpatch Camp for several days, talking to residents, attending camp committee meetings and dances, and watching Collins tactfully promote his concept of limited and guided self-government. Steinbeck and Collins travelled in the old bakery truck to nearby farms and ditch-side migrant settlements, and the

John Steinbeck, 1935. Photographer unknown.

author read the manager's regular reports to the Resettlement Administration's regional office in San Francisco. The reports, which included social and cultural observations on migrant life and individual anecdotes sometimes told in Okie dialect, were extraordinary documents. The News had already published excerpts from them, and Steinbeck eventually mined them for material for *The Grapes of Wrath*. In 1936 he used them to get beneath the surface of migrant life, to understand the deep despair and hopelessness that poverty and homelessness had created.

When Steinbeck returned from Arvin to his Los Gatos home, he wrote Collins to thank him "for one of the very fine experiences of a life." The two men remained in contact for another three years, Collins occasionally visiting Los Gatos and Steinbeck returning to the Central Valley for additional joint expeditions in what Collins called "the old pie wagon." The relationship was based as much on mutual advantage as on personal friendship. Steinbeck used the camp manager's experiences for real-life material, the grist of a writer's mill. And Collins used Steinbeck to publicize a deeply-felt cause, to awaken the citizenry to the migrants' plight. Jackson Benson said that Collins's most important contribution to *The Grapes of Wrath* was "to the spirit at the heart of the novel rather than to the details and color of its surface." Much the same can be said for Collins's influence on the 1936 News articles. Steinbeck recognized the camp manager's passion and promised, "I shall be very careful to do some good and no harm."

The articles are not only descriptive; they also contain specific policy recommendations. These, too, show the influence of Tom Collins. For example, Steinbeck calls for a vast expansion of the federal camp program. In both the articles and *The Grapes of Wrath*, the camp experience is the one bright exception to an otherwise gloomy account. Only in the camps does Steinbeck portray the migrants as somewhat in control of their lives, surviving with some dignity and self-respect. But by themselves, the camps were little more than palliatives. In *The Grapes of Wrath* the Joads are forced to leave the almost idyllic atmosphere of "Wheatpatch Camp" to find work. "We hate to go," Pa Joad explained. "Folks been so nice here-an' the toilets an' all. But we got to eat." Beyond the camps, then, Steinbeck advocated establishment of a state agricultural labor board to protect and promote the migrants' right to organize unions. Most important, he urged, federal and state authorities should begin a program of resettling the Okies on small family farms, perhaps on public land.

Both Steinbeck and Collins viewed the migrants as displaced Jeffersonian yeomen who needed and deserved their own small plots of land. Unfortunately, this ran counterto the whole direction of California agricultural history. The state's rural economy had never been dominated by small, Jeffersonian yeoman farmers. Instead, the Gold Rush allowed commercial producers to grow cash crops for instant urban markets in San Francisco and the mining camps. Completion of the trans-continental railroad in 1869 promoted a wheat boom in the Central Valley with large "bonanza farms" producing for international markets. By the 1870s, though a majority of California farms were small or middle-sized operations, the bulk of agricultural output was produced by a relatively few very large farms, some controlled by San Francisco businessmen. The shift to intensive fruit, vegetable and other specialty crop cultivation in the late nineteenth century did little to change that situation. If corporate agribusiness is a fairly new phenomenon in most of the United States, in 1936, when Steinbeck and Collins first toured Central Valley fields, it was already an established fact of life in California.

"Bindlestiffs," largely single, footloose men, made up most of the labor force of the great wheat farms of the 1870s and 1880s. But as the shift to fruits and vegetables increased the need for labor during the harvests and other intensive work periods, Chinese and other immigrants entered the farm labor market. Workers followed the varied crops up and down the state, creating the nation's first modern migrant agricultural labor force. When federal immigration restrictions affected the supply of Chinese labor, growers turned to Japan, southern Europe and even India. When further restrictions affected these areas, attention shifted to Mexico and the Philippines.

By 1935 the great wave of dust bowl migration was displacing many, though by no means all, of the immigrant, non-white laborers in California fields. From 1935 to 1938, between 300,000 and 500,000 Okies arrived in California. Poverty, land foreclosures and drought forced them out of Lower Plains states such as Texas, Arkansas, Missouri and, of course, Oklahoma. Ironically, federal programs designed to help farmers also contributed to the migration. The government paid property owners to take land out of production, thus displacingthousands of unneeded tenant farmers and sharecroppers.

Steinbeck and Collins believed that the dust bowl migration was fundamentally transforming ruralCalifornia society by changing the ethnic composition of the agricultural labor force. "Farm labor in California," Steinbeck predicted, "will be white labor, it will be American labor, and it will insist on a standard of living much higher than that which was accorded the foreign 'cheap labor.'" In an editorial accompanying the series, the News agreed, arguing that the dust bowl migrants "are Americans of the old stock. . . . They cannot be handled as the Japanese, Mexicans and Filipinos." Neither Steinbeck nor the News stooped to the crude racist vocabulary so common to the era, but both in effect were contending that only white Americans could successfully resist conditions which had regularly been imposed on non-whites and immigrants. As Steinbeck put it, the new arrivals "will refuse to accept the role of field peon, with attendant terrorism, squalor and starvation."

In fact, Okies proved less willing to organize and join unions than the Mexicans and Filipinos who had preceded them in California fields. The union organizing drives of largely immigrant workers in 193 3 and 1934, while ultimately failing, were far more successful than those of 1938 and 1939, when American-born Okies dominated the labor force. The dust bowl migrants still considered themselves independent farmers and found it difficult to give up their traditional rural individualism. When Tom Joad is urged to bring his family out on strike in *The Grapes of Wrath*, he replies, "Tonight we had meat. Not much but we had it. Think Pa's gonna give up his meat on account of other fellas?" Later in the novel, the death of his friend at the hands of anti-labor vigilantes moves Tom to become a union organizer. In the end, however, little came of the ambitious efforts to organize either white or non-white agricultural workers in California during the 1930s.

The most important opponent of unionization was the Associated Farmers, Inc., an organization of leading growers and their powerful corporate allies. The Associated Farmers also opposed the federal migrant camp program, fearing that the settlements would become centers of union organizing activity. In addition, local townspeople often resisted the establishment of migrant camps in their areas, arguing the camp residents would place a burden on schools, relief programs and other community institutions. Tom Collins and other Resettlement Administration officials were acutely aware that the towns also harbored substantial prejudice against the migrants; in one Central Valley community the local movie theater required

"Negroes and Okies" to sit in the balcony. In spite of such feelings, the Resettlement Administration and its successor the Farm Security Administration, eventually established fifteen California camps before the progam was liquidated after World War II. But even at their height in the late thirties, the settlements were still considered "demonstration projects" and served only a small fraction of the migrant population.

John Steinbeck and Tom Collins were dedicated New Deal liberals, yet the camps were the only New Deal program designed specifically to serve California farm laborers. Agricultural workers were not covered by Social Security, unemployment insurance, the minimum wage and the National Labor Relations Act. The New Deal was primarily a political response to the Depression, and unlike farm employers, the migrants had little political clout. While California growers obtained federal price supports for some products, legally enforced marketing orders for others, and massive government expenditures for irrigation projects, migrant laborers received a small, poorly funded camp program that never got beyond the "demonstration" stage.

Steinbeck recognized the migrants' political weakness and urged the establishment of a "militant and watchful organization" on their behalf. The group would be composed of "middle class people, workers, teachers, craftsmen and liberals," and it would fight for farm workers' rights against what Steinbeck called the "vigilanteism" and "fascism" of the Associated Farmers and its allies.

The Simon J. Lubin Society was exactly the kind of organization Steinbeck had in mind. Named for a progressive reformer who had fought for farm workers' rights, the Lubin Society struggled mightily to assist the migrants' cause. In 1938 Steinbeck allowed the group to publish his News articles in pamphlet form, under the title *Their*

Blood is Strong. In the same year, he uncharacteristically let his name be used by a similar group, the John Steinbeck Committee to Aid Agricultural Organization, formed by Hollywood actress (and future memberof Congress) Helen Gahagan Douglas. But the Lubin Society and the John Steinbeck Committee were no match for the Associated Farmers. Its allies in the state legislature blocked agricultural labor reforms proposed by liberal Governor Culbert Olson and his Director of Immigration and Housing, Carey McWilliams.

Setbacks such as these did not daunt Tom Collins or, for that matter, John Steinbeck. In early 1938 the two men were on the road again in rural California, travelling in the "old pie wagon" gathering material for a projected "big novel" on the Okie migration. They witnessed the devastating effects of that winter's floods on the Central Valley's "Little Oklahomas." Collins later described how he and Steinbeck worked "for forty-eight hours, and without food or sleep," helping "sick and half-starved people whose camps had been destroyed by the floods." "We couldn't speak to one another because we were too tired," Collins remembered, "yet we worked together as cogs in an intricate piece of machinery."

These and other experiences found their way into the letter and spirit of *Grapes ofWrath*, published in the spring of 1939. The novel took the nation's reading public by storm, going through ten printings between March and November of that year. The story's public exposure was dramatically increased by Darryl Zanuck's movie version, starring Henry Fonda. At one point Steinbeck, worried that Hollywood would soften or dilute the novel's message, asked Zanuck if he believed the story. The movie maker admitted that he had hired a detective agency to investigate whether the book had accurately depicted the migrants' plight. Zanuck told Steinbeck that "the conditions are much worse than you reported." At the author's suggestion,

Tom Collins. Photographer unknown.

Tom Collins was hired as a technical advisor for the film, and needless to say he argued for a realistic portrayal. Zanuck shot much of the movie in Collins's old stomping grounds, at the Weedpatch Camp and the countryside around Arvin. The film was released in early 1940, shortly before Steinbeck won the Pulitzer Prize.

Even the popularity of The Grapes ofWrath, however, did not produce significant public programs to assist the migrants. Foreign affairs and the coming U.S. involvement in World War II increasingly captured the nation's attention. By the end of 1940, reporter Ernie Pyle noted that the Okies no longer made headlines: "people sort of forgot them." A year later, the labor surplus of the Depression had been transformed into an extraordinary wartime shortage of workers. Migrants who were not subject to military service found well-paying jobs in California's booming shipyards, aircraft factories and other defense plants. The Joads and their fellow Okies ultimately found economic salvation, not in the small farms they dreamed of owning, but in urban industry fueled by billions of federal defense dollars.

California growers, desperate for labor, once again turned to Mexico. Hundreds of thousands of new workers crossed the border, many of them arriving under terms of the U.S. government's *Bracero* program. With the farm labor force no longer dominated by white Americans, little attention or sympathy was focused on social conditions in rural California. Not until the Delano Strike of 1965, in an era sensitized . by the Civil Rights movement, did issues raised in *The Grapes of Wrath* return to the broad public consciousness. And not until 1975 did the state legislature establish an Agricultural Labor Relations Board similar to the one Steinbeck advocated in 1936.

Back in December, 1939, after he had seen the movie version of the novel, John Steinbeck wrote to Tom Collins: "Saw the picture and it is swell. . . . You did a wonderful job . . ." Shortly thereafter, Collins dropped by Steinbeck's home in Las Gatos, only to find the house deserted. The novelist, recently separated from his wife, had moved on in his life and in his career, leaving the migrants and Tom Collins behind. The two men were never to meet again.

Although the series of articles collected in this volume was written over fifty years ago, Steinbeck's depiction of extreme poverty is not without relevancy today. In his time, homelessness and despair existed within the larger context of the Depression, and the general public was, for a while at least, genuinely touched by the suffering of migrants. In our time, prosperous Americans seem all too willing to accept the presence of homeless people. on the streets and a desperate "underclass" in the ghettoes. The sense of shock and indignation with which Steinbeck wrote these articles seems tragically absent in contemporary America. We can, then, still learn much from John Steinbeck's 1936 reports and from the activist spirit of his silent collaborator, Tom Collins, "who lived it."

REFERENCES:

Jackson Benson, *The True Adventures of John Steinbeck* (New York, Viking, 1984) and "Tom, Who Lived It: John Steinbeck and the Man from Weedpatch" *Journal of Modern Literature* (April, 1976)

Carey McWilliams, *Factories in the Field* (Boston, Little Brown, 1939)

Brian St. Pierre, *John Steinbeck, the California Years* (San Francisco, Chronicle Books, 1983)

Walter Stein, *California and the Dust Bowl Migration* (Westport, Greenwood, 1973)

Redding •

SACRAMENTO

VALLEY

Marysville •

Sacramento •

San Francisco

Santa Clara •

Modesto
• (Stanislaus County)
• Ceres

• Los Gatos

• Watsonville

Monterey

• Salinas   Fresno •

SAN JOAQUIN

VALLEY

Bakersfield
• (Kern County)
• Arvin

• Nipomo

Los Angeles •

IMPERIAL
VALLEY

San Diego •

1

AT THIS SEASON OF THE YEAR, when California's great crops are coming into harvest, the heavy grapes, the prunes, the apples and lettuce and the rapidly maturing cotton, our highways swarm with the migrant workers, that shifting group of nomadic, poverty-stricken harvesters driven by hunger and the threat of hunger from crop to crop, from harvest to harvest, up and down the state and into Oregon to some extent, and into Washington a little. But it is California which has and needs the majority of these new gypsies. It is a short study of these wanderers that these articles will undertake. There are at least 150,000 homeless migrants wandering up and down the state, and that is an army large enough to make it important to every person in the state.

To the casual traveler on the great highways the movements of the migrants are mysterious if they are seen at all, for suddenly the roads will be filled with open rattletrap cars loaded with children and with dirty bedding, with fire-blackened cooking utensils. The boxcars and gondolas on the railroad lines will be filled with men. And then, just as suddenly, they will have disappeared from the main routes. On side roads and near rivers where there is little travel the squalid, filthy squatters' camp will have been set up, and the orchards will be filled with pickers and cutters and driers.

The unique nature of California agriculture requires that these migrants exist, and requires that they move about. Peaches and grapes, hops and cotton cannot be harvested by a resident population of laborers. For example, a large peach orchard which requires the work of 20 men the year round will need as many as 2000 for the brief time of picking and packing. And if the migration of the 2000 should not occur, if it should be delayed even a week, the crop will rot and be lost.

Thus, in California we find a curious attitude toward a group that makes our agriculture successful. The migrants are needed, and they are hated. Arriving in a district they find the dislike always meted out by the resident to the foreigner, the outlander. This hatred of the stranger occurs in the whole range of human history, from the most primitive village form to our own highly organized industrial farming. The migrants are hated for the following reasons, that they are ignorant and dirty people, that they are carriers of disease, that they increase the necessity for police and the tax bill for schooling in a community, and that if they are allowed to organize they can, simply by refusing to work, wipe out the season's crops. They are never received into a community nor into the life of a community. Wanderers in fact, they are never allowed to feel at home in the communities that demand their services.

Let us see what kind of people they are, where they come from, and the routes of their wanderings. In the past they have been of several races, encouraged to come and often imported as cheap labor;

Chinese in the early period, then Filipinos, Japanese and Mexicans. These were foreigners, and as such they were ostracized and segregated and herded about.

If they attempted to organize they were deported or arrested, and having no advocates they were never able to get a hearing for their problems. But in recent years the foreign migrants have begun to organize, and at this danger signal they have been deported in great numbers, for there was a new reservoir from which a great quantity of cheap labor could be obtained.

The drought in the middle west has driven the agricultural populations of Oklahoma, Nebraska and parts of Kansas and Texas westward. Their lands are destroyed and they can never go back to them. Thousands of them are crossing the borders in ancient rattling automobiles, destitute and hungry and homeless, ready to accept any pay so that they may eat and feed their children. And this is a new thing in migrant labor, for the foreign workers were usually imported without their children and everything that remains of their old life with them.

They arrive in California usually having used up every resource to get here, even to the selling of the poor blankets and utensils and tools on the way to buy gasoline. They arrive bewildered and beaten and usually in a state of semi-starvation, with only one necessity to face immediately, and that is to find work at any wage in order that the family may eat.

And there is only one field in California that can receive them. Ineligible for relief, they must become migratory field workers.

Because the old kind of laborers, Mexicans and Filipinos, are being deported and repatriated very rapidly, while on the other hand the river of dust bowl refugees increases all the time, it is this new kind of migrant that we shall largely consider.

The earlier foreign migrants have invariably been drawn from a peon class. This is not the case with the new migrants. They are small farmers who have lost their farms, or farm hands who have lived with the family in the old American way. They are men who have worked hard on their own farms and have felt the pride of possessing and living in close touch with the land. They are resourceful and intelligent Americans who have gone through the hell of the drought, have seen their lands wither and die and the top soil blow away; and this, to a man who has owned his land, is a curious and terrible pain.

And then they have made the crossing and have seen often the death of their children on the way. Their cars have been broken down and been repaired with the ingenuity of the land man. Often they patched the worn-out tires every few miles. They have weathered the thing, and they can weather much more for their blood is strong.

They are descendants of men who crossed into the middle west, who won their lands by fighting, who cultivated the prairies and stayed with them until they went back to desert. And because of their tradition and their training, they are not migrants by nature. They are gypsies by force of circumstances.

In their heads, as they move wearily from harvest to harvest, there is one urge and one overwhelming need, to acquire a little land again, and to settle on it and stop their wandering. One has only to go into the squatters' camps where the families live on the ground and have no homes, no beds and no equipment; and one has only to look at the strong purposeful faces, often filled with pain and more often, when they see the corporation-held idle lands, filled with anger, to know that this new race is here to stay and that heed must be taken of it.

It should be understood that with this new race the old methods of repression, of starvation wages, of jailing, beating and intimidation are not going to work; these are American people. Consequently we must meet them with understanding and attempt to work out the problem to their benefit as well as ours.

It is difficult to believe what one large speculative farmer has said, that the success of California agriculture requires that we create and maintain a peon class. For if this is true, then California must depart from the semblance of democratic government that remains here.

The names of the new migrants indicate that they are of English, German and Scandanavian descent. There are Munns, Holbrooks, Hansens, Schmidts. And they are strangely anachronistic in one way: Having been brought up in the prairies where industrialization never penetrated, they have jumped with no transition from the old agrarian, self-containing farm where nearly everything used was raised or manufactured, to a system of agriculture so industrialized that the man who plants a crop does not often see, let alone harvest, the fruit of his planting, where the migrant has no contact with the growth cycle.

And there is another difference between their old life and the new. They have come from the little farm districts where democracy was not only possible but inevitable, where popular government, whether practiced in the Grange, in church organization or in local government, was the responsibility of every man. And they have come into the country where, because of the movement necessary to make a living, they are not allowed any vote whatever, but are rather considered a properly unpriviledged class.

Let us see the fields that require the impact of their labor and the districts to which they must travel. As one little boy in a squatters' camp said, "When they need us they call us migrants, and when we've picked their crop, we're bums and we got to get out."

There are the vegetable crops of the Imperial Valley, the lettuce, cauliflower, tomatoes, cabbage to be picked and packed, to be hoed and irrigated. There are several crops a year to be harvested, but there is not time distribution sufficient to give the migrants permanent work.

The orange orchards deliver two crops a year, but the picking season is short. Farther north, in Kern County and up the San Joaquin Valley, the migrants are needed for grapes, cotton, pears, melons, beans and peaches.

In the outer valley, near Salinas, Watsonville, and Santa Clara there are lettuce, cauliflowers, artichokes, apples, prunes, apricots. North of San Francisco the produce is of grapes, deciduous fruits and hops. The Sacramento Valley needs masses of migrants for its asparagus, its walnuts, peaches, prunes, etc. These great valleys with their intensive farming make their seasonal demands on migrant labor.

A short time, then, before the actual picking begins, there is the scurrying on the highways, the families in open cars hurrying to the ready crops and hurrying to be first at work. For it has been the habit of the growers associations of the state to provide by importation, twice as much labor as was necessary, so that wages might remain low.

Hence the hurry, for if the migrant is a little late the places may all be filled and he will have taken his trip for nothing. And there are many things that may happen even if he is in time. The crop may be late, or there may occur one of those situations like that at Nipomo last year when twelve hundred workers arrived to pick the pea crop only to find it spoiled by rain. All resources having been used to get to the field, the migrants could not move on; they stayed and starved until government aid tardily was found for them.

And so they move, frantically, with starvation close behind them. And in this series of articles we shall try to see how they live and what kind of people they are, what their living standard is, what is done for them and to them, and what their problems and needs are. For while California has been successful in its use of migrant labor, it is gradually building a human structure which will certainly change the State, and may, if handled with the inhumanity and stupidity that have characterized the past, destroy the present system of agricultural economics.

2

THE SQUATTERS' CAMPS ARE LOCATED all over California. Let us see what a typical one is like. It is located on the banks of a river, near an irrigation ditch or on a side road where a spring of water is available. From a distance it looks like a city dump, and well it may, for the city dumps are the sources for the material of which it is built. You can see a litter of dirty rags and scrap iron, of houses built of weeds, of flattened cans or of paper. It is only on close approach that it can be seen that these are homes.

Here is a house built by a family who have tried to maintain a neatness. The house is about 10 feet by 10 feet, and it is built completely of corrugated paper. The roof is peaked, the walls are tacked to a wooden frame. The dirt floor is swept clean, and along the irrigation ditch or in the muddy river the wife of the family scrubs clothes without soap and tries to rinse out the mud in muddy water. The spirit of this family is not quite broken, for the children, three of them, still have clothes, and the family possesses three old quilts and a soggy, lumpy mattress. But the money so needed for food cannot be used for soap nor for clothes.

With the first rain the carefully built house will slop down into a brown, pulpy mush; in a few months the clothes will fray off the children's bodies while the lack of nourishing food will subject the whole family to pneumonia when the first cold comes.

Five years ago this family had fifty acres of land and a thousand dollars in the bank. The wife belonged to a sewing circle and the man was a member of the grange. They raised chickens, pigs, pigeons and vegetables and fruit for their own use; and their land produced the tall corn of the middle west. Now they have nothing.

If the husband hits every harvest without delay and works the maximum time, he may make four hundred dollars this year. But if anything happens, if his old car breaks down, if he is late and misses a harvest or two, he will have to feed his whole family on as little as one hundred and fifty.

But there is still pride in this family. Wherever they stop they try to put the children in school. It may be that the children will be in a school for as much as a month before they are moved to another locality.

Here, in the faces of the husband and his wife, you begin to see an expression you will notice on every face; not worry, but absolute terror of the starvation that crowds in against the borders of the camp. This man has tried to make a toilet by digging a hole in the ground near his paper house and surrounding it with an old piece of burlap. But he will only do things like that this year. He is a newcomer and his spirit and decency and his sense of his own dignity have not been quite wiped out. Next year he will be like his next door neighbor.

This is a family of six; a man, his wife and four children. They live in a tent the color of the ground. Rot has set in on the canvas so that the flaps and the sides hang in tatters and are held together with bits of rusty baling wire. There is one bed in the family and that is a big tick lying on the ground inside the tent.

They have one quilt and a piece of canvas for bedding. The sleeping arrangement is clever. Mother and father lie down together and two children lie between them. Then, heading the other way; the other two children lie, the littler ones. If the mother and father sleep with their legs spread wide, there is room for the legs of the children.

There is more filth here. The tent is full of flies clinging to the apple box that is the dinner table, buzzing about the foul clothes of the children, particularly the baby; who has not been bathed nor cleaned for several days. This family has been on the road longer than the builder of the paper house. There is no toilet here, but there is a clump of willows nearby where human feces lie exposed to the flies—the same flies that are in the tent.

Two weeks ago there was another child, a four year old boy. For a few weeks they had noticed that he was kind of lackadaisical, that his eyes had been feverish. They had given him the best place in the bed, between father and mother. But one night he went into convulsions and died, and the next morning the coroner's wagon took him away. It was one step down.

They know pretty well that it was a diet of fresh fruit, beans and little else that caused his death. He had no milk for months. With this death there came a change of mind in his family. The father and mother now feel that paralyzed dullness with which the mind protects itself against too much sorrow and too much pain.

And this father will not be able to make a maximum of four hundred dollars a year any more because he is no longer alert; he isn't quick at piece-work, and he is not able to fight clear of the dullness that has settled on him. His spirit is losing caste rapidly.

The dullness shows in the faces of this family, and in addition there is a sullenness that makes them taciturn. Sometimes they still start the older children off to school, but the ragged little things will not go; they hide in ditches or wander off by themselves until it is time to go back to the tent, because they are scorned in the school.

The better-dressed children shout and jeer, the teachers are quite often impatient with these additions to their duties, and the parents of the "nice" children do not want to have disease carriers in the schools.

The father of this family once had a little grocery store and his family lived in back of it so that even the children could wait on the counter. When the drought set in there was no trade for the store any more.

This is the middle class of the squatters' camp. In a few months this family will slip down to the lower class. Dignity is all gone, and spirit has turned to sullen anger before it dies.

The next door neighbor family of man, wife and three children of from three to nine years of age, have built a house by driving willow branches into the ground and wattling weeds, tin, old paper and strips of carpet against them. A few branches are placed over the top to keep out the noonday sun. It would not turn water at all. There is no bed. Somewhere the family has found a big piece of old carpet. It is on the ground. To go to bed the members of the family lie on the ground and fold the carpet up over them.

The three year old child has a gunny sack tied about his middle for clothing. He has the swollen belly caused by malnutrition.

He sits on the ground in the sun in front of the house, and the little black fruit flies buzz in circles and land on his closed eyes and crawl up his nose until he weakly brushes them away.

They try to get at the mucous in the eye-corners. This child seems to have the reactions of a baby much younger. The first year he had a little milk, but he has had none since.

He will die in a very short time. The older children may survive. Four nights ago the mother had a baby in the tent, on the dirty carpet. It was born dead, which was just as well because she could not have fed it at the breast; her own diet will not produce milk.

After it was born and she had seen that it was dead, the mother rolled over and lay still for two days. She is up today, tottering around. The last baby, born less than a year ago, lived a week. This woman's eyes have the glazed, far-away look of a sleep walker's eyes.

She does not wash clothes any more. The drive that makes for cleanliness has been drained out of her and she hasn't the energy. The husband was a share-cropper once, but he couldn't make it go. Now he has lost even the desire to talk. He will not look directly at you for that requires will, and will needs strength. He is a bad field worker for the same reason. It takes him a long time to make up his mind, so he is always late in moving and late in arriving in the fields. His top wage, when he can find work now; which isn't often, is a dollar a day.

The children do not even go to the willow clump any more. They squat where they are and kick a little dirt. The father is vaguely aware that there is a culture of hookworm in the mud along the river bank. He knows the children will get it on their bare feet. But he hasn't the will nor the energy to resist. Too many things have happened to him. This is the lower class of the camp.

This is what the man in the tent will be in six months; what the man in the paper house with its peaked roof will be in a year, after his house has washed down and his children have sickened or died, after the loss of dignity and spirit have cut him down to a kind of sub-humanity.

Helpful strangers are not well-received in this camp. The local sheriff makes a raid now and then for a wanted man, and if there is labor trouble the vigilantes may burn the poor houses. Social workers, survey workers have taken case histories. They are filed and open for inspection. These families have been questioned over and over about their origins, number of children living and dead. The information is taken down and filed. That is that. It has been done so often and so little has come of it.

And there is another way for them to get attention. Let an epidemic break out, say typhoid or scarlet fever, and the country doctor will come to the camp and hurry the infected cases to the pest house. But malnutrition is not infectious, nor is dysentery, which is almost the rule among the children.

The county hospital has no room for measles, mumps, whooping cough; and yet these are often deadly to hunger-weakened children. And although we hear much about the free clinics for the poor, these people do not know how to get the aid and they do not get it. Also, since most of their dealings with authority are painful to them, they prefer not to take the chance.

This is the squatters' camp. Some are a little better, some much worse. I have described three typical families. In some of the camps there are as many as three hundred families like these. Some are so far from water that it must be bought at five cents a bucket.

And if these men steal, if there is developing among them a suspicion and hatred of well-dressed, satisfied people, the reason is not to be sought in their origin nor in any tendency to weakness in their character.

31

3

When in the course of the season the small farmer has need of an influx of migrant workers he usually draws from the squatters' camps. By small farmer I mean the owner of the five to 100-acre farm, who operates and oversees his own farm.

Farms of this size are the greatest users of labor from the notorious squatters camps. A few of the small farms set aside little pieces of land where the workers may pitch their shelters. Water is furnished, and once in a while a toilet. Rarely is there any facility for bathing. A small farm cannot afford the outlay necessary to maintain a sanitary camp.

Furthermore, the small farmers are afraid to allow groups of migrants to camp on their land, and they do not like the litter that is left when the men move on. On the whole, the relations between the migrants and the small farmers are friendly and understanding.

In many of California's agricultural strikes the small farmer has sided with the migrant against the powerful speculative farm groups.

The workers realize that the problem of the small farmer is not unlike their own. We have the example in the San Joaquin Valley two years ago of a small farmer who sided with the workers in the cotton strike.

The speculative farm group, which is closely tied up with the power companies determined to force this farm from opposition by cutting off the power necessary for irrigation. But the strikers surrounded and held the power pole and refused to allow the current to be shut off. Incidents of this nature occur very frequently.

The small farmer, then, draws his labor from the squatters' camps and from the state and federal camps, which will be dealt with later. On the other hand the large farms very often maintain their camps for the laborers.

The large farms in California are organized as closely and are as centrally directed in their labor policy as are the industries and shipping, the banking and public utilities. Indeed such organizations as Associated Farmers, Inc. have as members and board members officials of banks, publishers of newspapers and politicians; and through close association with the State Chamber of Commerce they have interlocking associations with shipowners' associations, public utilities corporations and transportation companies.

Members of these speculative farm organizations are of several kinds—individual absentee owners of great tracts of land, banks that have acquired land by foreclosure, for example the tremendous Bank of America holdings in the San Joaquin Valley and incorporated farms having stockholders, boards of directors and the usual corporation approach. These farms are invariably run by superintendents whose policies with regard to labor are directed from above. But the power of these organizations extends far beyond the governing of their own lands.

It is rare in California for a small farmer to be able to plant and mature his crops without loans from banks and finance companies. And since these banks and finance companies are at once members of the powerful growers' associations, and at the same time the one source of crop loans, the force of their policies on the small farmer can readily be seen. To refuse to obey is to invite foreclosure or a future denial of the necessary crop loan.

These strong groups, then, do not necessarily represent the general feeling toward labor; but being able to procure space in newspapers and on the radio, they are able, not only to represent themselves as the whole body of California farmers, but are actually able to impose their policies on a great number of the small farms.

The ranches operated by these speculative farmers usually have houses for their migrant laborers, houses for which they charge a rent of from three to 15 dollars a month. On most of the places it is not allowed that a worker refuse to pay the rent. If he wants to work, he must live in the house, and the rent is taken from his first pay.

Let us see what this housing is like, not the $15 houses which can only be rented by field bosses (called pushers), but the three to five dollar houses forced on the laborers.

The houses, one-room shacks usually about 10 by 12 feet, have no rug, no water, no bed. In one corner there is a little iron wood stove. Water must be carried from a faucet at the end of the street. Also at the head of the street there will be either a dug toilet or a toilet with a septic tank to serve 100 to 150 people. A fairly typical ranch in Kern County had one bath house with a single shower and no heated water for the use of the whole block of houses, which had a capacity of 400 people.

The arrival of the migrant on such a ranch is something like this—he is assigned a house for his family; he may have from three to six children, but they must all live in the one room. He finds the ranch heavily policed by deputized employes.

The will of the ranch owner, then, is law; for these deputies are always on hand, their guns conspicuous. A disagreement constitutes resisting an officer. A glance at the list of migrants shot during a single year in California for "resisting an officer" will give a fair idea of the casualness of these "officers" in shooting workers.

The new arrival at the ranch will probably be without funds. His resources have been exhausted in getting here. But on many of the great ranches he will find a store run by the management at which he can get credit.

Thus he must work a second day to pay for his first, and so on. He is continually in debt. He must work. There is only one piece of property which is worth attaching for the debt, and that is his car; and while single men are able to get from harvest to harvest on the railroads and by hitch-hiking, the man with a family will starve if he loses his car. Under this threat he must go on working.

In the field he will be continually attended by the "pusher," the field boss, and in many cases a pacer. In picking, a pacer will be a tree ahead of him. If he does not keep up, he is fired. And it is often the case that the pacer's row is done over again afterwards.

On these large ranches there is no attempt made for the relaxation or entertainment of the workers. Indeed any attempt to congregate is broken up by the deputies for it is feared that if they are allowed to congregate they will organize, and that is the one thing the large ranches will not permit at any cost.

The attitude of the employer on the large ranch is one of hatred and suspicion, his method is the threat of the deputies' guns. The workers are herded about like animals. Every possible method is used to make them feel inferior and insecure. At the slightest suspicion that the men are organizing they are run from the ranch at the points of guns. The large ranch owners know that if organization is ever effected there will be the expense of toilets, showers, decent living conditions and a raise in wages.

The attitude of the workers on the large ranch is much that of the employer, hatred and suspicion. The worker sees himself surrounded by force. He knows that he can be murdered without fear on the part of the employer, and he has little recourse to law. He has taken refuge in a sullen, tense quiet. He cannot resist the credit that allows him to feed his family, hut he knows perfectly well the reason for the credit.

There are a few large ranches in California which maintain "model houses" for the workers, neatly painted buildings with some conveniences. These ranches usually charge a rent of $5 a month for a single-room house and pay 33 1/3 per cent less than the prevailing wage.

The labor policy of these absentee-directed large farms has created the inevitable result. Usually there are guards at the gates, the roads are patrolled, permission to inspect the premises is never given.

It would almost seem that having built the repressive attitude toward the labor they need to survive, the directors were terrified of the things they have created. This fear dictates an increase of the repressive method, a greater number of guards and a constant suggestion that the ranch is armed to fight.

Here, as in the squatters' camps, the dignity of the men is attacked. No trust is accorded them. They are surrounded as though it were suspected that they would break into revolt at any moment. It would seem that a surer method of forcing them to revolt could not be devised. This repressive method results inevitably in flares of disorganized revolt which must be put down by force and by increased intimidation.

The large growers' groups have found the law inadequate to their uses; and they have become so powerful that such charges as felonious assault, mayhem and inciting to riot, kidnapping and flogging cannot be brought against them in the controlled courts.

The attitude of the large growers' associations toward labor is best stated by Mr. Hugh T. Osburne, a member of the Board of Supervisors of Imperial County and active in the Imperial Valley Associated Farmers group. Before the judiciary committee of the California Assembly he said: "In Imperial Valley we don't need this criminal syndicalism law. They have got to have it for the rest of the counties that don't know how to handle these matters. We don't need it because we have worked out our own way of handling these things. We won't have another of these trials. We have a better way of doing it. Trials cost too much."

"The better way," as accepted by the large growers of the Imperial Valley, includes a system of terrorism that would be unusual in the Fascist nations of the world. The stupid policy of the large grower and the absentee speculative farmer in California has accomplished nothing but unrest, tension and hatred. A continuation of this approach constitutes a criminal endangering of the peace of the state.

4

THE FEDERAL GOVERNMENT, realizing that the miserable condition of the California migrant agricultural worker constitutes an immediate and vital problem, has set up two camps for the moving workers and contemplates eight more in the immediate future. The development of the camps at Arvin and at Marysville makes a social and economic study of vast interest.

The present camps are set up on leased ground. Future camps are to be constructed on land purchased by the Government. The Government provides places for tents. Permanent structures are simple, including washrooms, toilets and showers, an administration building and a place where the people can entertain themselves. The equipment at the Arvin camp, exclusive of rent of the land, costs approximately $18,000.

At this camp, water, toilet paper and some medical supplies are provided. A resident manager is on the ground. Campers are received on the following simple conditions: (1) That the men are bona fide farm people and intend to work, (2) that they will help to maintain the cleanliness of the camp and (3) that in lieu of rent they will devote two hours a week towards the maintenance and improvement of the camp.

The result has been more than could be expected. From the first, the intent of the management has been to restore the dignity and decency that had been kicked out of the migrants by their intolerable mode of life.

In this series the word "dignity" has been used several times. It has been used not as some attitude of self-importance, but simply as a register of a man's responsibility to the community. A man herded about, surrounded by armed guards, starved and forced to live in filth loses his dignity; that is, he loses his valid position in regard to society, and consequently his whole ethics toward society. Nothing is a better example of this than the prison, where the men are reduced to no dignity and where crimes and infractions of the rule are constant.

We regard this destruction of dignity, then, as one of the most regrettable results of the migrant's life, since it does reduce his responsibility and does make him a sullen outcast who will strike at our Government in any way that occurs to him.

The example at Arvin adds weight to such a conviction. The people in the camp are encouraged to govern themselves, and they have responded with simple and workable democracy. The camp is divided into four units. Each unit, by direct election, is represented in a central governing committee, an entertainment committee, a maintenance committee and a Good Neighbors committee. Each of these members is elected by the vote of his unit, and is recallable by the same vote. The manager, of course, has the right of veto,

39

but he practically never finds it necessary to act contrary to the recommendations of the committee.

The result of this responsible self-government has been remarkable. The inhabitants of the camp came there beaten, sullen and destitute. But as their social sense was revived they have settled down. The camp takes care of its own destitute, feeding and sheltering those who have nothing with their own poor stores. The central committee makes the law's that govern the conduct of the inhabitants.

In the year that the Arvin camp has been in operation there has not been any need for outside police. Punishments are the restrictions of certain privileges such as admission to the community dances, or for continued anti-social conduct, a recommendation to the manager that the culprit be ejected from the camp.

A works committee assigns the labor to be done in the camp, improvements, garbage disposal, maintenance and repairs. The entertainment committee arranges for the weekly dances, the music for which is furnished by an orchestra made up of the inhabitants. So well do they play that one orchestra has been lost to the radio already. This committee also takes care of the many self-made games and courts that have been built.

The Good Neighbors, a woman's organization, takes part in quilting and sewing projects, sees that destitution does not exist, governs and watches the nursery; where children can be left while the mothers are working in the fields and in the packing sheds. And all of this is done with the outside aid of one manager and one part-time nurse. As experiments in natural and democratic self-government, these camps are unique in the United States.

In visiting these camps one is impressed with several things in particular. The sullen and frightened expression that is the rule among the migrants has disappeared from the faces of the Federal camp inhabitants. Instead there is a steadiness of gaze and a self-confidence that can only come of restored dignity.

The difference seems to lie in the new position of the migrant in the community. Before he came to the camp he had been policed, hated and moved about. It had been made clear that he was not wanted.

In the Federal camps every effort of the management is expended to give him his place in society. There are no persons on relief in these camps.

In the Arvin camp the central committee recommended the expulsion of a family which applied for relief. Employment is more common than in any similar group for, having something of their own, these men are better workers. The farmers in the vicinity seem to prefer the camp men to others.

The inhabitants of the Federal camps are no picked group. They are typical of the new migrants. They come from Oklahoma, Arkansas and Texas and the other drought states. Eighty-five per cent of them are former farm owners, farm renters or farm laborers. The remaining 15 per cent includes painters, mechanics, electricians and even professional men.

When a new family enters one of these camps it is usually dirty, tired and broken. A group from the Good Neighbors meets it, tells it the rules, helps it to get settled, instructs it in the use of the sanitary facilities; and if there are insufficient blankets or shelters, furnishes them from its own stores.

The children are bathed and cleanly dressed and the needs of the future canvassed. If the children have not enough clothes the community sewing circle will get busy immediately. In case any of the family are sick the camp manager or the part-time nurse is called and treatment is carried out.

These Good Neighbors are not trained social workers, but they have what is perhaps more important, an understanding which grows from a likeness of experience. Nothing has happened to the newcomer that has not happened to the committee.

A typical manager's report is as follows: "New arrivals. Low in foodstuffs. Most of the personal belongings were tied up in sacks and were in a filthy condition. The Good Neighbors at once took the family in hand, and by 10 o'clock they were fed, washed, camped, settled and asleep."

These two camps each accommodate about 200 families. They were started as experiments, and the experiments have proven successful. Between the rows of tents the families have started little gardens for the raising of vegetables, and the plots, which must be cared for after a 10 or 12-hours' day of work, produce beets, cabbages, corn, carrots, onions and turnips. The passion to produce is very great. One man, who has not yet been assigned his little garden plot, is hopefully watering a jimson weed simply to have something of his own growing.

The Federal Government, through the Resettlement Administration, plans to extend these camps and to include with them small maintenance farms. These are intended to solve several problems.

They will allow the women and children to stay in one place, permitting the children to go to school and the women to maintain the farms during the work times of the men. They will reduce the degenerating effect of the migrants' life, they will reinstil the sense of government and possession that have been lost by the migrants. Located near to the areas which demand seasonal labor, these communities will permit these subsistence farmers to work in the harvests, while at the same time they stop the wanderings over the whole state. The success of these Federal camps in making potential criminals into citizens makes the usual practice of expending money on tear gas seem a little silly.

The greater part of the new migrants from the dust bowl will become permanent California citizens. They have shown in these camps an ability to produce and to cooperate. They are passionately determined to make their living on the land. One of them said, "If it's work you got to do, mister, we'll do it. Our folks never did take charity and this family ain't takin' it now."

The plan of the Resettlement Administration to extend these Federal camps is being fought by certain interests in California. The arguments against the camps are as follows:

That they will increase the need for locally paid police. But the two camps already carried on for over a year have proved to need no locally paid police whatever, while the squatters' camps are a constant charge on the sheriff's offices.

The second argument is that the cost of schools to the district will be increased. School allotments are from the state and governed by the number of pupils. And even if it did cost more, the communities need the work of these families and must assume some responsibility for them. The alternative is a generation of illiterates.

The third is that they will lower the land values because of the type of people inhabiting the camps. Those camps already established have in no way affected the value of the land and the people are of good American stock who have proved that they can maintain an American standard of living. The cleanliness and lack of disease in the two experimental camps are proof of this.

The fourth argument, as made by the editor of The Yuba City Herald, a self-admitted sadist who wrote a series of incendiary and subversive editorials concerning the Marysville camp, is that these are the breeding places for strikes. Under pressure of evidence the

Yuba City patriot withdrew his contention that the camp was full of radicals. This will be the argument used by the speculative growers' associations. These associations have said in so many words that they require a peon class to succeed. Any action to better the condition of the migrants will be considered radical to them.

5

MIGRANT FAMILIES IN CALIFORNIA find that unemployment relief, which is available to settled unemployed, has little to offer them. In the first place there has grown up a regular technique for getting relief; one who knows the ropes can find aid from the various state and Federal disbursement agencies, while a man ignorant of the methods will be turned away.

The migrant is always partially unemployed. The nature of his occupation makes his work seasonal. At the same time the nature of his work makes him ineligible for relief. The basis for receiving most of the relief is residence.

But it is impossible for the migrant to accomplish the residence. He must move about the country He could not stop long enough to establish residence or he would starve to death. He finds, then, on application, that he cannot be put on the relief rolls. And being ignorant, he gives up at that point.

For the same reason he finds that he cannot receive any of the local benefits reserved for residents of a county. The county hospital was built not for the transient, but for residents of the county.

It will be interesting to trace the history of one family in relation to medicine, work relief and direct relief. The family consisted of five persons, a man of 50, his wife of 45, two boys, 15 and 12, and a girl of six. They came from Oklahoma, where the father operated a little ranch of 50 acres of prairie.

When the ranch dried up and blew away the family put its moveable possession in an old Dodge truck and came to California. They arrived in time for the orange picking in Southern California and put in a good average season.

The older boy and the father together made $60. At that time the automobile broke out some teeth of the differential and the repairs, together with three second-hand tires, took $22. The family moved into Kern County to chop grapes and camped in the squatters' camp on the edge of Bakersfield.

At this time the father sprained his ankle and the little girl developed measles. Doctors' bills amounted to $10 of the remaining store, and food and transportation took most of the rest.

The 15-year-old boy was now the only earner for the family. The 12-year-old boy picked up a brass gear in a yard and took it to sell. He was arrested and taken before the juvenile court, but was released to his father's custody. The father walked in to Bakersfield from the squatters' camp on a sprained ankle because the gasoline was gone from the automobile and he didn't dare invest any of the remaining money in more gasoline.

This walk caused complications in the sprain which laid him up again. The little girl had recovered from measles by this time, but her eyes had not been protected and she had lost part of her eyesight.

The father now applied for relief and found that he was ineligible because he had not established the necessary residence. All resources were gone. A little food was given to the family by neighbors in the squatters' camp. A neighbor who had a goat brought in a cup of milk every day for the little girl.

At this time the 15-year-old boy came home from the fields with a pain in his side. He was feverish and in great pain. The mother put hot cloths on his stomach while a neighbor took the crippled father to the county hospital to apply for aid. The hospital was full, all its time taken by bona fide local residents. The trouble described as a pain in the stomach by the father was not taken seriously.

The father was given a big dose of salts to take home to the boy. That night the pain grew so great that the boy became unconscious. The father telephoned the hospital and found that there was no one on duty who could attend to his case. The boy died of a burst appendix the next day.

There was no money. The county buried him free. The father sold the Dodge for $30 and bought a $2 wreath for the funeral. With the remaining money he laid in a store of cheap, filling food—beans, oatmeal, lard. He tried to go back to work in the fields. Some of the neighbors gave him rides to work and charged him a small amount for transportation.

He was on the weak ankle too soon and could not make over 75¢ a day at piece-work, chopping. Again he applied for relief and was refused because he was not a resident and because he was employed. The little girl, because of insufficient food and weakness from measles, relapsed into influenza.

The father did not try the county hospital again. He went to a private doctor who refused to come to the squatters' camp unless he were paid in advance. The father took two days' pay and gave it to the doctor who came to the family shelter, took the girl's temperature, gave the mother seven pills, told the mother to keep the child warm and went away. The father lost his job because he was too slow.

He applied again for help and was given one week's supply of groceries.

This can go on indefinitely. The case histories like it can be found in their thousands. It may be argued that there were ways for this man to get aid, but how did he know where to get it? There was no way for him to find out.

California communities have used the old, old methods of dealing with such problems. The first method is to disbelieve it and vigorous- ly to deny that there is a problem. The second is to deny local respon- sibility since the people are not permanent residents. And the third and silliest of all is to run the trouble over the county borders into another county. The floater method of swapping what the counties consider undesirables from hand to hand is like a game of medicine ball.

A fine example of this insular stupidity concerns the hookworm situation in Stanislaus County. The mud along water courses where there are squatters living is infected. Several business men of Modesto and Ceres offered as a solution that the squatters be cleared out. There was no thought of isolating the victims and stopping the hookworm.

The affected people were, according to these men, to be run out of the county to spread the disease in other fields. It is this refusal of the counties to consider anything but the immediate economy and profit of the locality that is the cause of a great deal of the unsolvable quality of the migrants' problem. The counties seem terrified that they may be required to give some aid to the labor they require for their harvests.

According to several Government and state surveys and studies of large numbers of migrants, the maximum a worker can make is $400 a year, while the average is around $300, and the large minimum is $150 a year. This amount must feed, clothe and transport whole families.

Sometimes whole families are able to work in the fields, thus making an additional wage. In other observed cases a whole family, weakened by sickness and malnutrition, has worked in the fields, making less than the wage of one healthy man. It does not take long at the migrants' work to reduce the health of any family. Food is scarce always, and luxuries of any kind are unknown.

Observed diets run something like this when the family is making money:

Family of eight—Boiled cabbage, baked sweet potatoes, creamed carrots, beans, fried dough, jelly, tea.

Family of seven—Beans, baking-powder biscuits, jam, coffee.

Family of six—Canned salmon, cornbread, raw onions.

Family of five—Biscuits, fried potatoes, dandelion greens, pears.

These are dinners. It is to be noticed that even in these flush times there is no milk, no butter. The major part of the diet is starch. In slack times the diet becomes all starch, this being the cheapest way to fill up. Dinners during lay-offs are as follows:

Family of seven—Beans, fried dough.

Family of six—Fried cornmeal.

Family of five—Oatmeal mush.

Family of eight (there were six children)—Dandelion greens and boiled potatoes.

It will be seen that even in flush times the possibility of remaining healthy is very slight. The complete absence of milk for the children is responsible for many of the diseases of malnutrition. Even pellagra is far from unknown.

The preparation of food is the most primitive. Cooking equipment usually consists of a hole dug in the ground or a kerosene can with a smoke vent and open front. If the adults have been working 10 hours in the fields or in the packing sheds they do not want to cook. They will buy canned goods as long as they have money, and when they are low in funds they will subsist on half-cooked starches.

The problem of childbirth among the migrants is among the most terrible. There is no prenatal care of the mothers whatever, and no possibility of such care. They must work in the fields until they are physically unable or, if they do not work, the care of the other children and of the camp will not allow the prospective mothers any rest.

In actual birth the presence of a doctor is a rare exception. Sometimes in the squatters camps a neighbor woman will help at the birth. There will be no sanitary precautions nor hygienic arrangements. The child will be born on newspapers in the dirty bed. In case of a bad presentation requiring surgery or forceps, the mother is practically condemned to death. Once born, the eyes of the baby are not treated, the endless medical attention lavished on middle-class babies is completely absent.

The mother, usually suffering from malnutrition, is not able to produce breast milk. Sometimes the baby is nourished on canned milk until it can eat fried dough and cornmeal. This being the case, the infant mortality is very great.

The following is an example: Wife of family with three children. She is 38; her face is lined and thin and there is a hard glaze on her eyes. The three children who survive were born prior to 1929, when the family rented a farm in Utah. In 1930 this woman bore a child which lived four months and died of "colic."

In 1931 her child was born dead because "a han' truck fulla boxes run inta me two days before the baby come." In 1932 there was a miscarriage. "I couldn't carry the baby 'cause I was sick." She is ashamed of this. In 1933 her baby lived a week. "Jus' died. I don't know what of." In 1934 she had no pregnancy She is also a little ashamed of this. In 1935 her baby lived a long time, nine months.

"Seemed for a long time like he was gonna live. Big strong fella it seemed like." She is pregnant again now. "If we could get milk for um I guess it'd be better." This is an extreme case, but by no means an unusual one.

6

THE HISTORY OF CALIFORNIA'S IMPORTATION and treatment of foreign labor is a disgraceful picture of greed and cruelty. The first importations of large groups consisted of thousands of Chinese, brought in as cheap labor to build the trans-continental railroads. When the roads were completed a few of the Chinese were retained as section hands, but the bulk went as cheap farm labor.

The traditional standard of living of the Chinese was so low that white labor could not compete with it. At the same time the family organization allowed them to procure land and to make it produce far more than could the white men. Consequently white labor began a savage warfare on the coolies. Feeling against them ran high and culminated in riots which gradually drove the Chinese from the fields, while immigration laws closed the borders to new influxes.

The Japanese were the next people encouraged to come in as cheap labor, and the history of their activities was almost exactly like that of the Chinese: A low standard of living which allowed them to accumulate property while at the same time they took the jobs of white labor. And again there were riots and land laws and closed borders. The feeling against the Japanese culminated in the whole "yellow peril" literature which reached its peak just before the war. The Japanese as a threat to white labor were removed. Some of them had acquired land, some went to the cities, and large numbers of them were moved or deported. The Japanese farm laborers, although unorganized, developed a kind of spontaneous organization which made them less tractable than the Chinese had been.

But, as usual, the nature of California's agriculture made the owners of farm land cry for peon labor. In the early part of the century another source of cheap labor became available. Mexicans were imported in large numbers, and the standard of living they were capable of maintaining depressed the wages of farm labor to a point where the white could not compete. By 1920 there were 80,000 foreign-born Mexicans in California. The opening of the intensive farming in the Imperial Valley and Southern California made necessary the use of this cheap labor.

And at about this time the demand for peon labor began to come more and more from the large growers and the developing shipper-growers. When the imposition of a quota was suggested, the small farmers (five to 20 acres) had no objection to the restriction, and 66 per cent were actively in favor of the quota.

The large grower, on the other hand, was opposed to the quota. Seventy-eight per cent were openly opposed to any restriction on the importation of peon labor. With the depression, farm wages sank to such a low level in the southern part of the state that white labor could not exist on them. Fourteen cents an hour became the standard wage.

To the large grower the Mexican labor offered more advantages than simply its cheapness. It could be treated as so much scrap when it was not needed. Any local care for the sick and crippled could be withheld; and in addition, if it offered any resistance to the low wage or the terrible living conditions, it could be deported to Mexico at Government expense.

Recently, led by the example of the workers in Mexico, the Mexicans in California have begun to organize. Their organization in Southern California has been met with vigilante terrorism and savagery unbelievable in a civilized state.

Concerning these repressive activities of the large growers, a special commission's report to the National Labor Board has this to say: "Fundamentally, much of the trouble with Mexican labor in the Imperial Valley lies in the natural desire of the workers to organize.

"Their efforts have been thwarted or rendered ineffective by a well-organized opposition against them. . . . We uncovered sufficient evidence to convince us that in more than one instance the law was trampled under foot by representative citizens of Imperial Valley and by public officials under oath to support the law."

The report lists a number of such outrages. "Large numbers of men and women arrested but not booked . . . intimidation used to force pleas of guilty to felonious charges . . . bail was set so large that release was impossible." This report further says: "In our opinion, regular peace officers and civilians displayed pistols too freely, and the police unwarrantedly used tear gas bombs.

"We do not understand why approximately 80 officers found it necessary to gas an audience of several hundred men and women and children in a comparatively small one-story building while searching for three 'agitators.'"

The right of free speech, the right of assembly and the right of jury trial are not extended to Mexicans in the Imperial Valley.

This treatment of Mexican labor, together with the deportation of large groups and the plan of the present Mexican government for repatriating its nationals, is gradually withdrawing Mexican labor from the fields of California. As with the Chinese and Japanese, they have committed the one crime that will not be permitted by the large growers. They have attempted to organize for their own protection. It is probable that Mexican labor will not long be available to California agriculture.

The last great source of foreign labor to be furnished the California grower has been the Filipino. Between 1920 and 1929, 31,000 of these little brown men were brought to the United States, and most of them remained in California, a new group of peon workers. They were predominantly young, male and single. Their women were not brought with them. The greatest number of them found agricultural employment in Central and Northern California. Their wages are the lowest paid to any migratory labor.

As in the case of the Mexicans, Japanese and Chinese, the Filipinos have been subjected to racial discrimination. They are unique in California agriculture. Being young, male and single, they form themselves into natural groups of five, six, eight; they combine their resources in the purchase of equipment, such as autos. Their group life constitutes a lesson in economy.

A labor coordinator of SRA [The State Relief Administration] has said, "They often subsist for a week on a double handful of rice and a little bread."

These young men were not permitted to bring their women. At the same time the marriage laws of California were amended to include persons of the Malay race among those peoples who cannot intermarry with whites. Since they were young and male, the one outlet for their amorous energies lay in extra-legal arrangements with

55

white women. This not only gained for them a reputation for immorality, but was the direct cause of many race riots directed against them.

They were good workers, but like the earlier immigrants they committed the unforgivable in trying to organize for their own protection. Their organization brought on them the usual terrorism.

A fine example of this was the vigilante raid in the Salinas Valley last year when a bunk house was burned down and all the possessions of the Filipinos destroyed. In this case the owner of the bunk house collected indemnity for the loss of his property. Although the Filipinos have brought suit, no settlement has as yet been made for them.

But the Filipino is not long to be a factor in California agriculture. With the establishment of the Philippine Islands as an autonomous nation, the 35,000 Filipinos in California have suddenly become aliens. The Federal Government, in cooperation with the Philippine government, has started a campaign to repatriate all of the Filipinos in California. It is only a question of time before this is accomplished.

The receding waves of foreign peon labor are leaving California agriculture to the mercies of our own people. The old methods of intimidation and starvation perfected against the foreign peons are being used against the new white migrant workers. But they will not be successful.

Consequently California agriculture must begin some kind of stock-taking, some reorganization of its internal economy. Farm labor in California will be white labor, it will be American labor, and it will insist on a standard of living much higher than that which was accorded the foreign "cheap labor."

Some of the more enlightened of the large growers argue for white labor on the ground "that it will not go on relief as readily as the Mexican labor has." These enthusiasts do not realize that the same pride and self-respect that deters white migrant labor from accepting charity and relief, if there is an alternative, will also cause the white American labor to refuse to accept the role of field peon, with its attendant terrorism, squalor and starvation.

Foreign labor is on the wane in California, and the future farm workers are to be white and American. This fact must be recognized and a rearrangement of the attitude toward and treatment of migrant labor must be achieved.

7

FROM ALMOST DAILY NEWS STORIES, from a great number of Government reports available to anyone who is interested, and from this necessarily short series of articles, it becomes apparent that some plan must be contrived to take care of the problem of the migrants. If for no humanitarian reason, the need of California agriculture for these people dictates the necessity of such a plan. A survey of the situation makes a few suggestions obvious. The following are offered as a partial solution of the problem:

Since the greatest number of the white American migrants are former farm owners, renters or laborers, it follows that their training and ambition have never been removed from agriculture. It is suggested that lands be leased; or where it is possible, that state and Federal lands be set aside as subsistence farms for migrants. These can be leased at a low rent or sold on long time payments to families of migrant workers.

Blocks of these subsistence farms should be located in regions which require an abundance of harvest labor. Small houses should be erected and the families settled, schools located so that the children can be educated. People who take these farms should be encouraged and helped to produce for their own subsistence fruits, vegetables and livestock—pigs, chickens, rabbits, turkeys and ducks.

Crops should be so arranged that they do not conflict with the demand for migratory labor. When the seasonal demand is on, the whole family should not be moved, but only the employable men. The subsistence farm could be managed during the harvest season by the women, the growing children and such unemployables as the old and the partially crippled.

In these communities a spirit of cooperation and self-help should be encouraged so that by self-government and a returning social responsibility these people may be restored to the rank of citizens. The expense of such projects should be borne by the Federal Government, by state and county governments, so that the community which requires the greatest number of seasonal workers should contribute to their well-being.

The cost of such ventures would not be much greater than the amount which is now spent for tear gas, machine guns and ammunition, and deputy sheriffs. Each of these subsistence districts should have assigned to it a trained agriculturist to instruct the people in scientific farming; and a spirit of cooperation should be encouraged so that certain implements such as tractors and other farm equipment might be used by the whole unit. Through the school or through the local board of health, medical attention should be made available, and instruction in sanitary measures carried on and enforced. By establishing these farms the problem of food during the five or six-month unemployment season would be solved, the degenerating influence of family moving would be removed and the education of the children would be assured.

There should be established in the state a migratory labor board with branches in the various parts of the state which require seasonal labor. On this board labor should be represented.

Local committees should, before the seasonal demand for labor, canvass the district, discover and publish the amount of labor needed and the wage to be paid. Such information should then be placed in the hands of the subsistence farmers and of the labor unions, so that the harvest does not become a great, disorganized gold rush with twice and three times as much labor applying as is needed.

It has long been the custom of the shipper-grower, the speculative farmer and the corporation farm to encourage twice as much labor to come to a community as could possibly be used. With an over-supply of labor, wages could be depressed below any decent standard. Such a suggested labor board (if it had a strong labor representation) would put a stop to such tactics.

Agricultural workers should be encouraged and helped to organize, both for their own protection, for the intelligent distribution of labor and for their self-government through the consideration of their own problems. The same arguments are used against the organizing of agricultural labor as were used 60 years ago against the organizing of the craft and skilled labor unions. It was argued then that industry could not survive if labor were organized. It is argued today that agriculture cannot exist if farm labor is organized. It is reasonable to believe that agriculture would suffer no more from organization than industry has.

It is certain that until agricultural labor is organized, and until the farm laborer is represented in the centers where his wage is decided, wages will continue to be depressed and living conditions will grow increasingly impossible until from pain, hunger and despair the whole mass of labor will revolt.

The attorney-general, who has been given power in such matters, should investigate and trace to its source any outbreak of the vigilante terrorism which is the disgrace of California. Inspiration for such outbreaks is limited to a few individuals. It should be as easy for an unbought investigation to hunt them down as it was for the Government to hunt down kidnapers. Since a government is its system of laws, and since armed vigilantism is an attempt to overthrow that system of laws and to substitute a government by violence, prosecution could be carried out on the grounds of guilt under the criminal syndicalism laws already on our statute books.

These laws have been used only against workers. Let them be equally used on the more deadly fascistic groups which preach and act the overthrow of our form of government by force of arms.

If these three suggestions could be carried out, a good part of the disgraceful condition of agricultural labor in California might be alleviated.

If, on the other hand, as has been stated by a large grower, our agriculture requires the creation and maintenance at any cost of a peon class, then it is submitted that California agriculture is economically unsound under a democracy. And if the terrorism and reduction of human rights, the floggings, murder by deputies, kidnappings and refusal of trial by jury are necessary to our economic security; it is further submitted that California democracy is rapidly dwindling away. Fascistic methods are more numerous, more powerfully applied and more openly practiced in California than any other place in the United States. It will require a militant and watchful organization of middle-class people, workers, teachers, craftsmen and liberals to fight this encroaching social philosophy, and to maintain this state in a democratic form of government.

The new migrants to California from the dust bowl are here to stay. They are of the best American stock, intelligent, resourceful; and, if given a chance, socially responsible. To attempt to force them into a peonage of starvation and intimidated despair will be unsuccessful. They can be citizens of the highest type, or they can be an army driven by suffering and hatred to take what they need. On their future treatment will depend which course they will be forced to take.

Walking from the mines to the lumber camps to the farms, the "bindlestiff" had long formed the backbone of California's migrant work force. Napa Valley, 1938. Photo by Dorothea Lange.

Families fleeing the bankrupt farms and dust storms of the midwest camped behind a billboard along Highway 99, San Joaquin Valley, 1938. Photo by Dorothea Lange.

*Oklahoma refugees reach the San Fernando Valley, near Los Angeles, 1935.
Photo by Dorothea Lange.*

Sharecropper from Oklahoma and family stalled on desert as they enter California, 1937.
Photo by Dorothea Lange.

Stopped by the side of the road. Date and photographer unknown.

Family in flight, 1935. Photo by Dorothea Lange.

Migrant camp under eucalyptus trees. Date and photographer unknown.

Water supply at a migrant camp.
Date and photographer unknown.

Camp for citrus workers, San Joaquin Valley, 1938. Photo by Dorothea Lange.

Winter rains at a migrant camp. Photo by Dorothea Lange.

Wife and child of migrant worker camped near Winters, Sacramento Valley, 1936
Photo by Dorothea Lange.

Family in Tulare County. Photo by Dorothea Lange.

Drinking water for field workers' families. Imperial Valley, 1935
Photo by Dorothea Lange.

Migrant camp on the outskirts of Marysville, 1936. Photo by Dorothea Lange.

Left: Oklahomans' camp on river bottom near Holtville, Imperial Valley, 1937. Photo by Dorothea Lange. Right: Migrant field workers' home on edge of a pea field. A family lived here throughout the winter. Imperial Valley, 1937. Photo by Dorothea Lange.

Family in a one-room shack, 1935. Photographer unknown.

Hooverville, Sacramento, Calif.
Ambitious but destitute families have formed
community of home-made homes.

"Hooverville" near Sacramento. Date and photographer unknown.

Entranceway to government camp, Marysville. Photo by Dorothea Lange.

Administration buildings at government camp, Marysville. Photo by Dorothea Lange.

Workers at a Farm Security Administration Camp, Calipatria, Imperial Valley, 1939.
Photo by Dorothea Lange.

A youngster named Evon Evanoff playing marbles at a mobile camp unit near Sacramento before the opening of a permanent camp, 1941. Photographer unknown.